"A tour de force through the landscape of desire, Kiara Letcher's *Oxblood* revels in the pulse of creation and being. This collection, named for the deep, purplish red color of dye made from ox's blood, is passionate, luxuriously fine. These poems are a place where X-file creatures crawl out of psyches in overheated rooms while someone reads your most private diary. Carnal, daring, lunar-ly maternal, Letcher's poems are spells that mix the depths and mysteries of life where 'lust tastes like cherry limeade.'"

— Elizabeth AI Powell, author of *Atomizer* (LSU Press)

"*Oxblood* blends of dark red with purple and brown undertones, pigments like dried rose petals as they fall onto the page. Kiara Nicole Letcher's collection voyeurs a lonely 'liminal luminous portal' of hunger through a 'dance of metamorphosis,' '[a] dance of all the destruction/ that has been gifted.'

Letcher mixes transformation, mourning, and witchcraft: 'the dye bleeds making murky circles/ distorted vision of violet.' Her words 'speak of all the unspeakable things.' This collection, once devoured, with its taste still on your tongue, illuminates '[t]he end of the spell/ climaxes with finding/ the hope of everything.' *Oxblood* is raw vitality of all human Experience."

—Bonnie Johnson-Bartee

"*Oxblood* comes on as a swarm of desires, its nimble speaker asking all sorts of pointed questions: 'Will you still love me if I moon rise too soon? / If I show you some werewolf ache?' These bold poems seek to secure a space for the self — however strange, however unsettling — to thrive. Kiara Nicole Letcher is a poet of depth and nuance, summoning us to bravery with her 'halo tipped back / heat you cannot reason with.'"

—Todd Robinson, author of *Mass for Shut-Ins*

Oxblood

Kiara Nicole Letcher

AGAPE
EDITIONS

BINGHAMTON, NY

Published by Agape Editions
https://agape-editions.com

Author photo by Kiara Nicole Letcher
Image appears by kind permission

Editor: Fox Henry Frazier
Designer: Sarah Reck

Library of Congress
Cataloguing-in-Publication Data
Oxblood // Kiara Nicole Letcher
Library of Congress Control Number 2024935824

Letcher, Kiara Nicole
ISBN 978-1-961862-99-9

9 8 7 6 5 4 3 2 1
FIRST EDITION

AGAPE
EDITIONS

For my mother, Lee Shanna and sister, Kaleah.

"Devour without guilt"— Margaret Atwood

"Feel your body closing, I can rip it open"—FKA Twigs

Contents

Fever Dream

Protect me from what I want.
Protect them from what I want.

There's a fly in my champagne coupe
the door is locked from the wrong side

Freshly squeezed stars and glitter all over the floor
freshly squeezed heart vessels and vermillion all over the ground
I once read that even an asteroid can be a celestial body

A drop of blood in fresh water pooling out
mercurial watercolor portrait of self
there are nights when something is happening
that should not be happening
a black swallowtail emerging and transforming
inside of a women's home

Vanish into emptiness
a hungry stillness beckons with airy hands

If I was a werewolf I would tear this mourning to pieces
at night leave my body skin, teeth, feet
peel them off like a wet bathing suit
leave them in the backyard limp

I would moan low
up there over in the ether
hovering in the violet heaven before twilight

Airy/breathlessly chilled/maybe
not really anywhere at all.

You don't need to be in pain to bleed

I.
Pull it up by the roots examine all decay
you are a voyeur

Mildew and earthworms

No one looks the way they usually do
inside their house
undressing their faces at night

No one looks the same
inside of their head
as they do on the outside
to the people they love
or better yet, strangers.

We are playing pretend
we are playing house
we were playing doctor

Burnt paper dolls and ceramic rot

II.
I question what I use to think I needed
the glamour of lust is my favorite trick
of the light

III.

I have a strange face and a stranger face
I rearrange my strange face
in brilliant magpie
I stretch and sketch details in pleasant
linen colors and peacock feathers

My stranger's face lives in the
basement
it scratches around and
sometimes I let it peep out
no one knows what It really looks like
if you glance
out of the corner of your eye
you might catch a glimpse

Something shifting among cellar
shadows

IV.

Can I have both—

The fleshy physical and a form I cannot hold?

Let's see what tomorrow brings
this dirt
ever damp
ever earth
ever transforming.

Oxblood Queen

Settling of sediment
deep plum stained lip
riddle drawn in rust
homage to the red clay
under my skin

I am sure footed
my ancestors flex their legs
as they watch me run up hills

Not looking back
is an exercise of the muscles
to not be brimmed with shame
is a choir of amazement

This map is stained
ripped at the edges
I want to go everywhere
be enchanting and fluid
with excitement
stargazing and never wilted

Eat the entire fucking
pomegranate
let out a low base growl
begin to dance like Ishtar
feeling the waves of my hips

a dance of all the destruction
that has been gifted

Drink me like a fountain cherry cola
before I go back into
my temptation shell.

Some October Night

This sweater is hot
take it off and
spread my body like fig jam
on the floor of this room.

Right now. With fucking urgency!
Put your hands on my waist
lay me down like a Ouija board
drink me like spiked cider
feel that slow burn
like a good horror movie or rich whiskey.

Something is happening that should not be happening...

In this house there is a door that will not lock

My mouth is always ajar
paradox unlimited

Melodrama syrupy
with buzzy honeycomb

I'll move like prairie fire until you want me.

Strawberry Fever

Bite the moan
      that feeds you

Whisper like rain
waves crashing together
  and breaking
     apart
     again

Fantasy cove and sea dazzler
something spectacular
soft serve ice cream melts
like a scream
down
                    hand

Bonfire from breast
heat shoots up
                            skyward.

Champagne on a Wednesday

Don't allow them to tell you that
your desires cheapen you.

Devour with your gaze
keep nothing in check
speak all of the unspeakable things
drape yourself in ornamentals

Put his fingers in your mouth
read a thousand books
run for miles
dance till you sweat
throw back your head
yelling at the night glory
telling the treetops your indiscretions

Turn face speckled with Swarovski gems
toward the rising sun.

I've Set Out All of the Traps For Us

I start to miss you right after you leave
at night I feel a deep throb
in that need spot
full to the brim with crave

You are holding my mouth wide open
in lust and embarrassment

Why are you seeing me so full and lush?
I see tarnished jewelry and half-eaten birthday cake

Don't look at me that way
don't watch me like that
with your hand on the throttle
and my trap door fully open.

Lift the shirt over your head, Let the roses fall out

Your eyes the color of hazy guava
kiss me wide and open
run the chili powder on your mouth

When you have nothing better to do
swallowing matches is a fun trick
how many things have you ruined?

You are lonely and I am lonely too
eat me like saffron
you are an escape artist and I am a stunt double
we are both lava lamps

Move to the synth of bees buzzing
tear into pulpy promises like the beginning of summer
your eyes the color of hazy guava
run the chili powder on your mouth.

I wrote your name in my diary

In my nightgown, I watch nightingales
fly through evening

Sad is the color of emptiness
sick is the smell of rot

My daydream of you
is probably not as you really are.

Cream Filled

Rub your mouth over glazed doughnut
sigh in inappropriate glutton
sugar coated heartache

Lust fiend you are left
sin swollen wading waist high into the riverbed
rubbing dirt on your breast from the flowerbed
dropping bits of mud and magic
from your hands

                                    Hello?
                            Are you still there?

It is 1am and I am
crawling to you
wandering my voice over absinthe chilled glasses
confessing grimy secrets

Paradise a toothache

I want what I cannot have
what a fantasy to be seen.

Feral

Wild thing, smell the hunt
perspiration/pheromones/viscera

I'm coming to you
electric and free
over woodsy zephyr
remember you cannot always
undo damage and hurt

Lift up machete

        Stop.

Right in your tracks.

I carry distance in my body

My good words and deeds vaporize

Villainous appetite always reappears
rising like steam on balmy summer mornings

Tigers stalking the sky like sunrise
keen claws
wild eyes.

I have inappropriate dreams all Pisces Season

Delusional euphoria
musky nectar
grab up the skirt
hand around neck
rug burn

Torn torrid
paper back novel

I need to climb

                                        out

of this pool

Apply melancholy lipstick
while looking into a mirror
backward

Scrub dark swelter from bedsheets

Open your jaws

                        release the Banshee.

Hold Out Your Tongue

Lust tastes like cherry limeade
heart massive and indulgent

I am caramel inside of a Valentine's Day heart

My feelings are the deep end of a swimming pool
leave me here with my heady escapism

Daydream soaking my lips
reverie the color of magenta breaking through trees

If you pull me back
do so by my throat.

Slide into toxic thought

Admire those visceral women
roots deep in their own elation

Watch the first few angry
fresh blades of grass
shove themselves through chilled
hard earth

I am botanical fuck up
my heart a shape shifter shuttering
in and out of throbbing love

In quiet moments I am honest with myself
I look at my goblin face
resist giving into grime

Create spring wreathes
out of ashes and tulips
pull stray strands of
sunlight from the
brilliance of day

This is a clean project to keep
a mind from tangling
with envy like ivy.

For Cookie

My Grandmother tells too many stories
I get that from her
I never want to say too much
but sometimes I cannot stop
it's as if another me has pulled
my mouth full and wide
letting dried rose petals fall out

A flood is a thing that makes me think of faeries
I miss my grandmother's house
the sweet earth that blankets the grass

My Mummum is the rabbit and the wild tree
the witch, the spider and the farm
the hot gritty earth

Her face is a gold sun coming up over the city
glowing onto sisters, ships, churches and streets

She sips sweet wine and tells me
of plants with deep roots
new dresses
men on horseback
gives me salt water taffy that I rip at with sharp teeth

Her hair used to be so long she could sit on it
when it was wet it was heavy and strained her neck

I consider her like that
all that long dark hair
now cropped short in waves of white
like gentle ocean foam

Someone is singing by The Waterfront
a song of palm trees and too many storms.

While Looking at J Crew clothes

I realize that even
when I am older
I will still wear dresses
and skirts above
the knee

God propagated
these legs for a reason.

Swallowtail Moth

A busted birthday gift
I am ripping my mind open

Chest unlocked
womb extending
and reaching

Moths pour into the streetlight

Lately there is always some lust
I am not allowed to thirst trap
my mouth trying to cram too many
rubies like so many
Maraschino jewels

I wish I was prettier.

Hunley Women

Listen— We have things to say
pick apart and examine

Look here
at this spider leg
chew on mint leaf

Phantasm almond eye
see how memories smile
so many silhouettes dancing into
the midnight

Crush plums with thought and fists
shot glass half full
cigar smoke rising

3am singing in
I love you
see you
understand.

If I start crying now
I'll never stop.

Wondrous Swoon

The need to come undone
press fingertips to zipper

A longing—
pines growing tall with yearning

A woman lounging in love
a mother in stunning pregnancy

Pining for morning or
thirsting for evening

The good news is that there's still
dewy light

Open mother wound
a firm

      push.

If I could be—

Soft beauty
you know...

                     two angels
                        kissing

lips barely
       touching

parted with sincerity
one breath into another's breath

                    creating spirit.

Bewitched

Illuminate floral fresh
insides

Promising
the beginning
scarlet of summer

Hold—

                                  Shudder

a thought

I forgot to close
that part of myself

Wait...

What was I saying?

Alchemist

Carry rebirth to the surface
recreation is always messy
remind yourself of this when you pull the Death Card
multiple times

There's a shivering in my pores
revival is the only option

Carry trauma like a tattoo
or a branding
feel it keloid.

Baby Spider

This is what spring in your soul must feel like
unlacing your boots and putting your feet
into pulsing turquoise waves

Your face bare without decoration
just in the state the God made you

Nature does not say sorry for being God

Everything is intentional

You are perfect
blossoming beauty

Do not take yourself for granted
nurse your naked body
in recluse silk
learn to catch creatures
unaware.

Let me Monsoon into my Cups

Bleeding dawn like a new mother
legs spread
pushing life through

Gateway

We endure then move through
liminal luminous portal.

My Warmest Intentions

It's what I would like to give
my bravest of spirits

Heart warm apple pie

Blackberries voluptuous and sticky
violaceous stained fingers

Braid and unbraid impossibility
the evaporation of a love story
floats skyward on a muggy day

Past lusts and loves
hear me when I say I am healing
web weaving
manifesting in cobra scales
and exfoliated skin.

Kith and Kin

Lean in and speak softly
your ear gently swallows
the secret
like whirlpool

If I show you this soot
and there is not a gasp
only a knowing like
the onset of May foxgloves
then I call you kindred.

Hell is being too high in a hot room
while someone reads your diary

Sorry for the unnecessary stories
for the need to go and say
weird shit all the time

Sorry for the strange X File creatures
who have crawled out
of my psyche

For the way they watch and scratch
from the other side of the valley
sing through the trees
in falsetto hypnotic trill

I want to be murky and mysterious
but I lack the ability to shut the fuck up.

A bird is stuck in my throat chakra.

This Is What Makes Us Girls
We All Look For Heaven —Lana Del Rey

—For Alli

I'm passing a note to you
lyrics to your favorite songs
folding it in half and half again
whispering some secret
that will make you laugh

What I want to ask is
"Why" did you leave early?
Will you pass a note back?

I picture you grinning
mouthing "love you"
walking away into

        sunlight.

Sandhills

Memorize Ursa Major
the pattern of clouds
the shape of so many constellations

If you were in the country,
they would be a purer white
more luminous
and easily identifiable

In the suburbs
they are a little dim
a little stifled, but still very much there.

Lonely Pink

Dear Time Traveler
go to the early 2000s

Tell her she is Bambi eyes,
swan feathers and cashmere baby.

Tell her to shut her ears
and close her eyes

Do not listen to them
call her other or
broken windchime.

Medicine

My hair rises like smoke stacks
curls a snarl

A dark and conflicting
history book

My skin is like earth pigmented umber
have you ever wished for straighter hair?

The courage for wrapping myself in affection

the Ace of Cups.

Trickster

The Coyotes sang against
the moon and I was the only one to hear
their lyrics full of athletic inflection

What a foul waste
that I was only a child
unable to understand their possession
only learned to hold my face
to the sky years later

In their vocals I felt and found
humans are just animals with souls
pushing love off a
steep
sharp
cliff.

Fawn

Fall through the floor
send your mom a letter
call her in the middle of the night

> *Help me, hold me!*
> *I am sad again, I am sad again, I am sad again!*

Get mad at her
listen to inky silence and phone static

I wish I had all of the money in the world
to help us lights up into act two
in a range rover and shiny golden rings

Are you listening to me?

Watching me drink chlorine
from the swimming pool?

Stumble into bushes in stilettos
trade one serial killer for another
slip on period stain
paint a mosaic.

The Spread: Past, Present, Future

The ecstasy
of the sun and its breath
intoxicates the very vibrations
of my skin

There is no devil here
only warm sand and
sunrise horizon

I am in Clearwater again
wearing my own golden halo
from my early laughter

Hang me upside in the mud
suspended in the terrorverse
no way out other than
to cloak myself in dirt and rock

Slice my life from callous love
this is me detaching
from the earth

Rolling something brassy
on my tongue.

Years of the Snake

Remember him saying

> *Hi, Snakes...*

Coil and uncoil
flex iridescent muscle

Others do not know the courage it took to summon
strength to push back
rather than fall

Unhinge
warp out of mind fuck

                                  Do you

understand?!

To strike
rather than slither

                                  on belly-

ache

                                  away.

Phantoms

Never stay quiet for too long
and some tell the most delicious stories.

9 of Swords

The air overheard is crisp
the sky covered in haze
someone is burning fall foliage
and dead summer grass

Last night I dreamt that I couldn't stop running
legs aching of acid

Snapshots or sticky notes to remember
your fantasies or disruptions

Notes on nature: A void or a dense forest
Lily of the Valley and vines

Photos on want: Sex and confetti
a tearing cry ripped open

Notes on beauty: A bouquet of red roses
layers of petals
rich luxuriant soil
a peony bush glimmering

Pull open desire
unsnap the buttons of its shirt
prize it open to show a 9 sword heart
head in hands again

I read that sometimes falling in love is much less
glamorous than it appears on TV

Butterfly into moth & butterfly into moth

I have many notes on transformation
but they all contradict themselves.

You cannot scrub me out

I am a blood stain
cheap Merlot headache pain

Hang on while my voice whispers like
steam and mist Poltergeists from a lake
rising up like hair standing on end

Non-symmetrical and fearful
I don't think I have much grace left
I have boiled my linens and washed my anger
hung on a clothesline

Weeping in my Sunday best
there is no time for softness.

Hello Haunts

All of the texts I never sent
and so many that I did send
constantly haunt me.

There is no fucking point if I can't show all this red

I put you on display
you, you, you
with my face in the mirror

You were wearing my face
and had those teeth like daggers

I showed you like a girls first cycle
the cut foot on a bed of coral
in shallow water

How will I get to the opulence without
wading waist deep in Oxblood?!

I see a reflection and
wonder
        whose is it?

Do you miss me when I'm gone?
and it's only a stranger's face?

I remember your voice
like crushed glass under my heel
or some watery vibration.

The Moon Over Open Coastline

You stood there looking at me
when you got a little too close
and gazed a little deeper you realized
I might bring you out to sea never to return

I didn't understand your insincerity
only understood the intensity of wanting you
only could comprehend the language of
desperation

You went and retreated landside

While I stayed lurking in the water
contained to all my tides of emotion
all my salt and cold
lunar pulling waxing and waning
seaweed wrapped legs
crowned in the hyper awareness of what
is at the bottom of the unforgiving
shadowy shipwrecked ocean floor

You looked briefly terrified
but also strangely sad

This is an oath—

I will envelope all my multitudes

with the passion and depth
that I wanted to envelope you

I will be psychic
full of urchin and chaos
sit comfortably in shadow self
escape to the euphoric ether

Lay my body down like Tarot cards
in that lunar space
where the depths of the sea
stretch reality.

Bad Mojo

Look for a mountain pass
or stream to flow homeward
while your eyes shine like
flicks of razor rock

I own cursed objects
       I know I do

Weathered wedding dress
white fabric full of stains
a map too faded to read

Bleary compact mirror.

Disruption

A fire, a fire, there's a fire outside of the house
a flood, a flood, there's a flood inside of the home

There are tears waltzing down the staircase
the plot is thick and the mood is swelling

What if I don't life raft away?

You are always angry

I never forget and my forgiveness
is only an old band-aid
covering a reopened scab.

Sister, I had a Nightmare where you needed my help

I watch you in the forest
with a lantern
hear you mummer profanities

You race those perfect people
to the trees edge

Stretch your arms out wide
in the darkness
you who have become so
skilled at being "other"

Werewolf goddess ready
you sway in emerald green
a dance of metamorphosis

Cracking cicada shell
that holds beauty that no one else
wants to see

Welcoming birth
your arms deep in the nether
ready to display
a warm shaking new
splendor.

When my son saw the cemetery for the first time:

No baby that is not a lake
it is a graveyard

On nights when the moon is
pregnant with light
it becomes a house party
of souls.

Motel Static

I told him I didn't need him
or this repeatedly rewound film

Packed our disputes in a box
listened to conspiracy theories flimsy
as tissue paper
regifted that shit to myself
over and over again

Cheap motel room TV static at 3am
showing the same gnashing teeth
grisly crimson weeping

Tuck into taut bedsheets
fold body in linen safety net
cradled in cotton breath

Spill pills that help with sleep
like dice, baby teeth
broken pearl earrings

Walk around on a tight rope of apologies
welcome the last wind chill
with satisfaction

Polish rib cage, dust off the frost
forget winter tree limbs scratching

at the window

Pray for spring and all its pastel smiling.

Casting a Spell

Spin in ethereal golden circles
stunning
      terrible
            isolated
kick up moss and river bed
a spill of sweat

Old divinity cast away

Now she's floating
in air scented with magnolia
aged plastic Mardi Gras beads around her neck

Leave a small bouquet of blooms
at the door of the Cinnamon
      Whiskey
Goddess

Think of her when you're in the throes
of exhilaration watching vespers
from the hotel floor

The end of the spell
climaxes with finding
the hope of everything.

Aquatic Fruit

There is deep purple here
grottos as eyes
bruises like eggplant

Days run into a series of
constant little knicks and jarring scars
when saltwater licks legs
all the little unnoticed cuts
come alive at once
with crimson resentment

Water knows and remembers
that moment of death
the moment of birth
with an intimacy like dark velvet
along skin

I have never been quiet
my words reverberate
thunder over chilly
looking glass

I pour out shades from my urn
watch them backstroke.

Lasagna

I'll cry into my pasta on another "date night"
and you'll watch in that self-righteous way

It's not your uncaring, your anger
or political ranting that I'm crying about
It's this trap, this quicksand
the maze never ending
the constant trip on the rug

A remembrance
is dinner burning again?!

You haven't made me sad
you've made me so pissed and fiery that
I'm burning from the inside

A torch, a tower
a roman fucking candle!

Sweetener

The air smells like snow
the air tastes like ice
Judas, Judas, Judas

I've hurt my own feelings again
reached in and squeezed
a little too hard
felt jammy ichor

       drip
drip
       dripping
some rung out washcloth

I want something I can't fucking have
my hands stretched so far apart
the skin between my fingers burn
like a rubber band stretched too thin

This glowering mind
a brightly lit neon sign
left on for too long

I have a sickness called hope
a feeling of eating too much cotton candy
sugary violence.

Better Things-Pamela Adlon

Do they want mothers to be unseen?

    Women to be ghosts after a certain age?

                                Then we'll haunt them.

Mourning After

Did they call you a slut?
Did they not know you were just lonely?

Screwdriver

I've never been called someone's Sunday morning
but I have been called a stupid fucking bitch
on a Sunday morning

I've been called a stupid fucking bitch
on a Sunday morning and afternoon and evening

I prize those words apart
wear them like cellophane
stuff them into my mouth like
Devil's Food cake.

The Witch said You Will Be OK

I went and had my oracle cards read

After the reading the witch gave me
a candle, oil, and a safety pin for a spell

I never performed the spell

Maybe that is why I am still tethered to
a blister I cannot heal.

I undressed my face for you

It hurts here, in this delicate place
I pointed to the cracked shell
prized it opened to viscous yolk

Shame lunges forward on grasshopper legs

My loss came with no golden embrace
or tether of closeness
I am without a bow for my gift
my face a bruised purple sky from all the cry

Vexing hurt left split open
palms like sliced tomatoes
red and demanding
there will be no cleaning of this contusion

We are all just broken pieces of mountain
waiting to avalanche

I am on the lookout for thunder
perched over a high cliff waiting
like a cloud that begins to
 exhale.

He Left You in The Basement

Hello, high tension
I live for her rage and big moods

This mood is busting a pumpkin skull
into tiny little pieces
it is saying assault or non-consensual
and maybe not laughing about it this time

Here is a slice of unsolicited advice...

If you have a sexual attraction
to destruction
do not unearth things
that are not meant to be uprooted
push to tell the truth to yourself
talk to mirrors and waterways
yell out the ghouls in your lungs
and the specters in your memory

Write these things in old photobooks
scribble them on fortune cookie paper

Let me impart an obvious secret—
there is no elevation in achieving
disastrous outcomes
do not turn back
to the echo you might hear

in a darkened tunnel

Maybe a harsh fact will help your heartache...

Your cherub face is gone
deal with that sorrowful truth
shed those old childhood books
pages on the ground
a trail of November leaves

Return golden harmony.

Tart

Consume cherry
     twist stem
run tongue over cut
isn't this pout cute
isn't this poolside
shimmer beautiful?

Iridescent dragonfly wings
still on the ground
something has happened that should not have happened

Grab under bathing suit
scrape knee

hit head against
        diving
           board

                  apply pressure to all wounds

Clench fist around words
     I don't want to
or simply
     I am drunk

No one sees aqua neon tears
under the lonely veil

Period blood on silk nightgown
sucker punch of hangover
your body
tearing down
the walls.

On the walk home alone

It is sleeting
your frozen face turned
toward the unsympathetic
wind

Walk through the door
smear off makeup
call him
      hang up the phone

write a text
     rewrite the text
hit send
         feel stupid

Lay on the carpet
in tempest soaked underwear
cry
sleep.

But will you still call me baby in the morning?

To be a beautiful woman and in love?

What a fucking dream.

Motel Cowboy

Silver dollar tongue
soul knitted from artificial light

My voice breaking like vodka bottle tumbling
from top shelf
I cried inky tears all over my
white dress

Pinprick of sadness after a party
fistfuls of lonely notes stuffed into
belly

Ritual irritation
absence of pleasure
cracks in our plaster

Seeing you
is choking on stone fruit
roots curving into
my stomach.

Pluck scream from air

No one feels the way you do
little girl cinnamon twist
who wishes on
moonbeam

The beasts always find the tender spots

Somewhere a blood rose
blooms

Vivid grinding molars
thrilling technicolor infection

You are morphed into something
looming
monstrous.

I Have a Great Thirst

Lick grit off sea cave

These ghosts are hungry
these birds have quiet hearts
I held a white dove and instead of

      Hallelujah
I yelled
      God Dammit!

Someone grab my good scissors
while I make something sacred
haunted by accident

The greatest thing I've ever crafted
is a family home set inside of a ghost story

Last night I dreamt I couldn't stop bleeding like an over ripe
mango

When I was younger, I once cut my birds wings too close to the
wick
it flinched and bled, and I felt bad
I learned to not cut where it hurts

      Cut over here instead

Revenge is doing all right
tell him you are doing all right except
for the thirst

Stick the papercut in your mouth
wait

It will be alright.

She Wore Blue Velvet

Hold my hand and eat
my laughter

Carry it in your cheek
as we walk through this
picket fence-lined street

There is a charming atmosphere to
this evening

I want to wear it like a mink coat

I know it can't last
I will be alone again tomorrow
or you will get too close and
I will have to put this out

Like a match searing fingertips.

Garden Hose

In this story dread overflows
like a lawn hose left on in the middle of July
all that pooling water late into dusk
sopping grass

Will you still love me if I moon rise too soon?
If I show you some werewolf ache?

...Something is happening, that should not be happening

Crying under the childhood swing set
halo tipped back
heat you cannot reason with

Bomb Pop sticky on your shorts

A summer stopped
dead on the ground.

The Shame Language

Feminine like papaya
mid menstrual cycle
a dragon breathing fire

Seraphim and mermaid teeth
hair like nets, catch and ensnare
feminine like papaya

Siren singing worship hymn, broken hymen
drink the gloaming heavens like sangria
a dragon breathing fire

Things I am in love with:
Neroli oil and Sandalwood
tobacco tasting wine with peppery undercurrent

Witchcraft how could I forget you
my love a steady thunderous heartbeat
a dragon breathing fire

I am not a fountain of temperance
I love being a woman
feminine like papaya
a dragon breathing fire.

A Goodbye Letter

I wield stories in my body
like so many knives on a
butcher's block

I am chilly and distant
also evergreen and abundant
mercurial watermelon heart
somewhere inside my body
is hot summer asphalt
to burn the soles or
melt strawberry ice cream

I release your clothes into warm water
the dye bleeds making murky circles
distorted vision of violet

This golden failure

                                spoken viciousness
Shhh...

I lay in bed thinking indigo thoughts
the ocean doesn't feel shame for being cold
the desert doesn't feel embarrassment for being scolding

I take a hot shower
wipe the mirror of fog
smear my reflection into
something abstract and bleary
maybe even
corrected.

Carousel Hotel

The sky holds stars like glistening
little teeth in its mouth

Perspiration from dancing
mystic afterglow

Smile unfolding like Louisiana daybreak.

Cannonball into Nightshade

I am still awake
conversing with a quartet of crickets
      tranced with hedonism.

I am Mother of Swords and Magician
cultivating my lush garden
split me open like sacred geometry
slippery
        peach

Fluorescent halo shined up bright
with a little too much poison

Sometimes I'm a cast away nymph
delicate doll bones
        loose change
other times a predator
huntress
            spill of blood

I think I'm the wolf
carrying faerie tales
in my burning belly
                roaming openly

Go deep into the basement
below the floor boards

where there are things you don't want to look at

Coppery smells attached to
memories like pennies in a
         wishing well

Impish cocktail of everything is great and confusing at once

Shimmy out of bathing suit
skinny dip
while I swell with stars.
light shines through little cookie cut outs
on my thighs

Reach my legs in the space where
I can become radiant

         Ripe as blood orange
                  soft

                           nutmeg
                           skin

Glitzy blue and deceiving omen
oleander braided into hair
mist and violet

Stretch in supine

Now I glide

         and smolder.

Thank You Notes

I listened to a lot of music and watched countless horror movies while creating this book. I thank all the artists who helped me set the mood and craft the melodrama for my poems to live within.

And so magical thanks go out to some of the following inspirations:

The hundreds of horror movies and shows I watched while writing this book. Especially, the following. A Wounded Fawn, The Love Witch, X, Hellbender, Blue Velvet, Brand New Cherry Flavor, Death Proof/Planet Terror, Better Things, Jawbreaker and Foxy Brown.

All the women on my Oxblood playlist I created. Your words, rage, sorrow and beats were instrumental while working on this book: Lana Del Rey, FKA Twigs, Beyonce, Megan Thee Stallion, Garbage, Hole, SZA, Stevie Nicks, Tinashe, Rhianna, Tayor Swift, Poppy and Elle King.

Love notes go to Francesca Lia Block. Your inspiration on using lush language will not be lost on fans of your work. Borrowed is the imagery of Blood Roses and Watermelon Hearts.

Many thanks to Sarah Reck, who created the cover (and interior) for Oxblood, and brought my vision to a beautiful smoky reality.

Bouquets of Flowers for Agape Editions! For Fox Henry Frazier and Jasmine An. Both of whom helped bring this book forth.

Thank you for your collaboration and enthusiasm for my melodrama and strangeness.

To my family for loving and supporting me. I wouldn't be a writer or have the opportunity to share my/our stories without you. I'm grateful to all of you.

To my beautiful friends who helped manifest this with me. Thank you for your friendship, beauty, long nights, and escapes. You are all in this book in some shape or form.

Acknowledgments

Thank you to the following publications in which these poems first appeared, some in earlier forms:

South Dakota Review
I Have a Great Thirst

Adelaide Magazine
There's a Fly in my Champagne Coupe
The door is locked from the wrong side
Swallowtail Moth
Trickster
He Left You In The Basement
I Undressed My Face For You

Alice Says Go Fuck Yourself
Some October Night

Plainsongs
9 of Swords
You Cannot Scrub Me Out

Every Writer
I've Set Out All The Traps For Us

Sad Girl's Club
A Goodbye Letter

Solstice Literary Magazine
The Shame Language

Querencia Press
Strawberry Fever
Lift the shirt over your head, Let the roes fall out
Years of the Snake

Laurel Review
Screwdriver

Mulberry Literary
Hold Out Your Tongue

About the Author

Kiara Nicole Letcher is the author of *Scream Queen* (The Orchard Street Press, 2019). Spinning lush imagery with magic and horror, she explores shame, want, and growth. She received her MFA from The University of Nebraska at Omaha in 2014.

Her work has appeared in *Green Mountains Review*, *South Dakota Review*, *Plainsongs Magazine*, *Querencia Press*, *Mulberry Literary*, *Solstice Literary Magazine* and *Alice Says Go Fuck Yourself*. Her work is forthcoming in *Laurel Review*.

You can find her at her website, kiaranicoleletcher.com or on Instagram @kiaranicolebang.

AGAPE
EDITIONS

Agape Editions is a literary micropress created in southern California, now located in upstate New York. We publish visionary literature.

Our name comes from the ancient Greek ἀγάπη (agápē), describing the joyous love that exists universally without seeking or expecting anything in return. Agape can be described as the bond between humans & the Numinous, but we believe it exists everywhere—manifested through the kindness of strangers, felt alone under a sky filled with aurora, made real through a moment of ecstatic meditation or deep connection with another.

A moment of Agape is a moment in which you feel yourself fully—in the broader context of the universe at large.

Agape is about finding the strength & courage to remain open-hearted, in a world that doesn't always encourage or reward an open heart. Our notions of the sacred & the Numinous span wide swaths of experience—private epiphanies; shared ecstasies; moments of intimacy; sublime revelation; cultural identity; spiritual traditions as conduit for survival. The psychic, the occult, the supernatural. The divinity of the natural world. Wild love. Fascinating scientific discovery. Mind-blowing technological advancement. *Fernweh*. The thrill of exploration. Sacred feminine rage.

We are profoundly uninterested in attempting to dictate the parameters of spiritual experience. We want to feel through you & your writing what's holy to you & why.

Imagine: awakening, breathless, in the thick of night. You've been dreaming of William Blake's Tyger-burning-bright & all its terrifying beauty. & now, from somewhere in the surrounding darkness, you can hear its quiet breathing.

Welcome to Agape Editions.